# The Speaking Heart

## PRIYANKA ATHIA

notionpress.com

INDIA · SINGAPORE · MALAYSIA

ISBN  979-8-89067-824-9

I dedicate this book to the memory of my late father (papa) and Grandfather (Nana ji), who taught me throughout my life and loved me unconditionally. Their encouragement, guidance and unwavering belief in me were instrumental in shaping the person I am today.

My father (papa) was my hero and mentor. He taught me the value of hard work, perseverance and integrity. He listened to my thoughts and aspirations and provided me with a safe space to express myself. He encouraged me to pursue my dreams and never gave up on me, even when I faltered.

My grandfather (Nana ji) was my confidante and friend. He showed me kindness, generosity and empathy and his wisdom and humor continue to inspire me.

Although they are no longer with me, their memory and legacy live on through this book. I hope that it serves as a tribute to their love and support, and that they are proud of the person I have become.

Thank you, Papa and Nana ji. I love you both and I miss you <3. And also thanks to my Radhe-Krishan and universe for everything.

# Contents

CONTENTS

# प्रेम

# LOVE

# प्रेम और आज़ादी

तुम जो मेरे हुए!

तो आज़ाद पंछी के जैसे उड़ना,

हवाएं जो तुमसे करें सवाल!

तो जवाब मुझसे लें ये कहना।

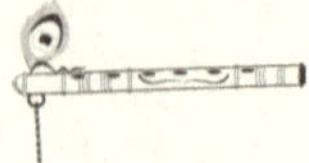

# Love and Freedom

Loving is not binding in a contract. Love is freedom. The power and strength of love in the form of "security" with which one can roam anywhere freely, the power of love with 'support' with which one can do anything freely. The strength of love, which provides "emotional support," enables one to withstand any heartbreak without restraint. The ability to effortlessly find serenity in any loudness through the use of "devotion" to love.

# प्रेम और हम

तुम कहते हो मैं अपना ख्याल रखूं!

की अनजान हो तुम! फ़क़त मुझमें तुम ही हो!

फिर कहते हो तुम मैं दुनिया को भी तो देखूं!

की अनजान हो तुम! फ़क़त मेरी दुनिया तुम ही हो!

की अब तुम सुनो,गर! अनजान हो तुम।

ये तेर मेर का ताना बाना नहीं,

फ़क़त "हम" ही सुनो और कहो तुम।

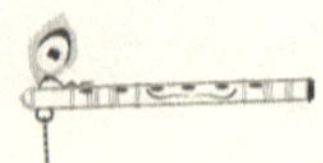

# Love and We

When we love someone, we try to make them feel more loved by doing little things for them.

We keep on doing without expecting anything. No matter how much busy we are, we always manage to give ideal time to them, No matter what the situations are, We always try to be there for them in the first place. No matter what the conditions are, we always try to plan little surprises for them to see that beautiful smile on their face.

Their smiles are our happiness.
Their sufferings are our pain.
Their hard work makes us proud.

Our soul is connected to them in a way that we start finding them inside us, we start feeling 'they as us'. That beautiful journey of two, where the destination is only one soul i.e.; "WE".

# प्रेम और रूह

दिल की बात हो और तर्जुमानी अबसार करें,

तो कैसे जिस्म से पहले इश्क़ रूह में ना ढले।


**तर्जुमानी** - satisfaction

**अबसार** - eyes

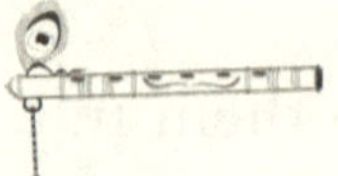

# Love and Soul

The Love of soul doesn't seek the love of body and it makes you remain loyal for your whole life.

If you are finding love in the body, then maybe you will be successful in it, but it will be for a temporary time as the body is temporary. If people say "LOVE IS GOD ", then how someone can find God without awaking the soul.

And if love is possible with the body, then one day the body must die, but how love can die inside the lover. Love can never die if the soul was loved, it can be more, it can be less, but if you have loved someone truthfully then the flame of love will never die.

# प्रेम और महसूस

जाने दो ये सब बातें!

की तुम मेरे हो,मैं तुम्हारा हूं,

बस ये बताओ! की मेरे दर्द में होने से तुम्हारा दिल कहता है तुम्हें " मैं तकलीफ़ में हूं"।

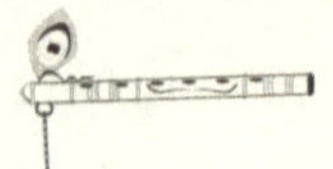

# Love and Feel

Yes! Love is comfort, Love is calmness, Love is relief, but it also brings pain with it. Pain of your loved ones, when they are in pain. When you are attached to them soulfully, you are not able to ignore it. You feel their pain as if it's your pain. Where your loved ones tries to get over that pain, at same time you try twice as hard to find the solution. You don't look after losses, droppings, benefits or profits later that you will eventually experience. Your heart and your mind only know how to find out a way to take away the pain of your loved ones. And if this is not happening, then saying "I love you",

"I am yours", in words, never matters.

# प्रेम और चुप्पी

की अब अहसास लबरेज़ है,

लबों को बोलने की जरूरत नहीं,

तुम्हारे पास दिल है ? तो महसूस कर लो!

हर्ज! हमें दिल खोलने की इजाज़त नहीं।

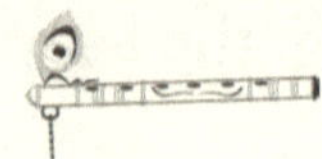

# Love and Silence

One person, to whom we reach out first in any problem.

One person, whom we remember first in any celebration. That's only because emotionally we are so attached to that person, that even if we are not explaining to them, they will understand us. They are so into us that they know how we will react in the next moment better than us. They know our anger, love, anxiety, and every emotion as well as how to handle it. But that only happens when the two souls are so tangled that two bodies will make one soul.

# प्रेम और प्राथमिकता

तू जरूरत नहीं जरूरी है!

ये! कह देते तुम!

तो मेरे लिए क्या जरूरी रह जाता ?

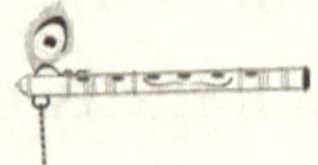

# Love and Priority

Soul connection always finds its pleasure in love, care, respect! We always need to remind our loved ones that they are important, they always come first. May be sometimes being busy in life it will be tough to share same quality time, collect beautiful moments with them, where our loved ones will start feeling that now they are not "important", they will start losing excitement, happiness, joy which they ever felt with us. The point where they will start feeling insecure and at same time point arguments will start, interests will suddenly change, misunderstanding will start, unwanted fights and maybe drastic end! Which was never thought of, So try to spent some good time with loved ones, little efforts to bring smiles, a good discussions without judgements.

# प्रेम और सहारा

ख़ुदा की बात का इशारा, जो कायनात करती है,

सूखी जमीन पे जो काम बरसात करती है,

वैसी मोहब्बत है तुम्हारी!

तबीब और ताबीज़ दोनों ही बन जाती है,

रोग है या बला,

बिन बोले ही रूह का हाल जान जाती है।

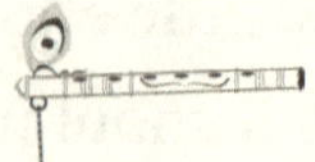

# Love and Support

Care, respect and then comes the love. Every time your heart knows to whom it should reach? To share each and every emotion, feeling, and even those words which are really hard to explain. Keep that "whom" with trust and loyalty.

# प्रेम और आदत

मुझे जागने की आदत है या तुम्हें मुझे जगाने की ?

की अब मैं लिखने भी बैठूं कहीं!

तो तुम्हारे ख़यालों को आदत हो गई है,

मेरे ख़याल मिटाने की।

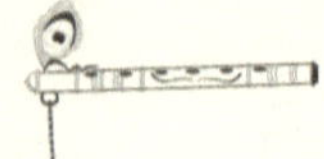

# Love and Habit

Unnaturally, someone can force themself to sit idle physically but how can they make their minds idle at the same time?

It's hard to control the thoughts of mind but it is possible to make those thoughts constant by focusing on "one". That one can be your "love", "a goal to achieve something" which doesn't take you away from anything but takes you nearer to yourself.

# प्रेम और एक

मुराद दिल की और दुआ दिल से!

महज़ एक।

बात चांद की और गुफ़्तगू चांद से,

महज़ आसमान तेरा मेरा एक।

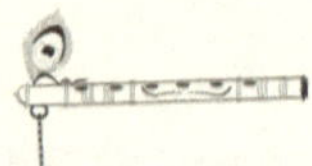

# Love and One

Someone is everything and that everything is one. The life of two people revolves around each other. And that 'each 'and 'other' is also one.

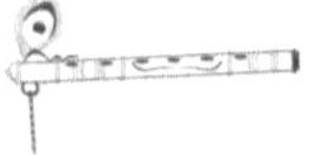

# प्रेम और सादगी

सजना संवरना सादगी एक तरफ़ी है,

उसकी झुकीं नज़रों में भी खुबसूरती है।

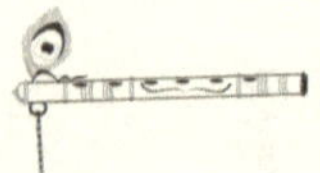

# Love and Simplicity

Be beautiful by your heart first,

Then only everything will be beautiful.

Keep your soul pure first,

Then only every other thing will look faithful.

Keep the spirit of being natural and positive first,

Then only every other thing will look real.

# प्रेम और वादा

अभी तो रिश्ता बना है,

निभाना बाकी है।

चार दिन की चांदनी में सब सोना-सोना है,

ज़रा वक़्त तो दीजिए हुज़ूर,

अभी इस रिश्ते को हीरे सा चमकाना बाकी है।

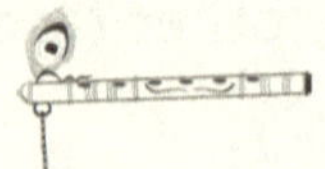

# Love and Promise

Bringing new relationships into your life is one of the easiest tasks. But living in it, giving time to it, nourishing it, is the toughest job. So certainly, we should set up new relations but don't forget that all are important.

# प्रेम और भरोसा

सबूत हो वो भी सब्त!

जी! मोहब्बत है ना की इमारत।

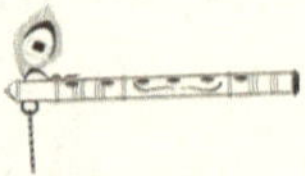

# Love and Trust

Kindness, faith, prayers, love, emotions, affection, decency, belief and blessings don't have proof!

These cannot be expressed but can be only felt if the listener holds true intentions.

# प्रेम और प्रयास

चलो आपकी छोटी सी बात और हमारी लंबी रात!

वो रात निकल जाए आपकी बात समझने में,

और आपको सुकून आ जाए हमें नजर-अंदाज़ करने में।

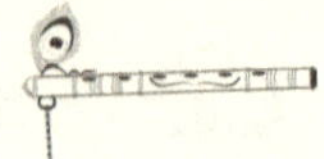

# Love and Efforts

Sometimes a stage arrives, when you are the only one who is trying to put in all efforts just because your partner is stuck between some unwanted situations that no one has ever thought of. And due to all these unwanted situations, he/she is not able to love you like before. At this time if we will start raising questions over the love bond that we share, then we are actually creating one more unwanted situation for them. Where we can be their support to settle down everything again, in the same state we can also be the reason for whole loss in their life.

The choice is ours.

# प्रेम और कल्पना

हम तुम्हारे आशिक़ नहीं होते,

चलो! तुम कातिल सा मुस्कुराना छोड़ दो!

हम जो कह दे फ़िदा हैं तुम पे,

तो यूं करो तुम की नज़रें मिलाना छोड़ दो!

तह कर लिया आज से हमने बेकसूर रहेंगे हम,

बस! तुम सादगी और हुस्न को उलझाना छोड़ दो!

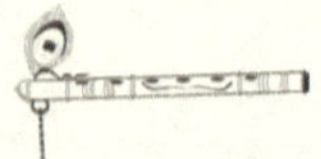

# Love and Imagination

"Love" is a fancy world till both persons are equally dipped in the ocean of love.

But when a situation of rejection happens it really hurts. Although no one is responsible for this situation. 'One' is saying the truth of not holding any feelings and 'another' is trying hard to control the feelings. Feeling of truly loving 'someone', caring for 'someone', accepting 'someone' the way they are and above all,feeling a soulful connection with that 'someone' when they are around or not. That 'another' is trying best to respect the decision that had been given.

Yes! That is why? Every time that person requests God, either to keep that "someone" in life or completely as far as possible. Because even the glimpse, the voice, the movements.

# प्रेम और दर्द

ज़ख्म जिस्म का हो तो भर ही जाता है,

ये दर्द तो रूह का है जो कब्र तक साथ जाता है।

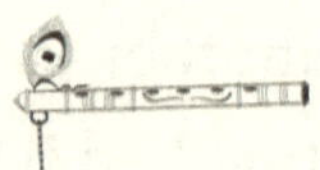

# Love and Pain

A wound can be healed, but unanticipated pain brought on by someone we love deeply is intolerable and cannot ever be healed or forgotten. Choose to be "kind" since life is brief and unpredictable.

# प्रेम और सब कुछ

सजदा नसीब ना हमें खुदा का!

राब्ता आपकी आँखों से दिल का यूँ हुआ!

कि अब! सजदा भी आप ही,

नसीब भी आप ही,

बेशतर! खुदा भी आप ही।

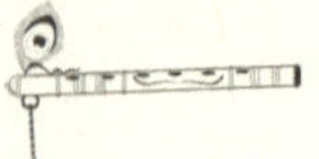

# Love and Everything

Love is sky.

Love is earth.

Love is fire.

Love is water.

Love is force.

Five precious elements of this universe when added become one i.e. God.

Love is "GOD". Love is a way to "GOD" Where truthfulness, stillness, purity, indubitable, everything is just for "one". Two bodies with "One" soul.

Seeking "God" in love and "LOVE" in God.

# प्रेम और कुछ भी नहीं

नुमाइश उन्स की,

कीमत कुर्बानी कुर्बत को,

बावजूद के! सिफर रहा आशिक के लिए, खुब!


नुमाइश - Numaish - Exhibition

उन्स - uns - Love

कीमत - Qeemat - cost

कुर्बानी - Qurbani - sacrifice

कुर्बत - Qurbat - Nearness

सिफर - sifr - Zero

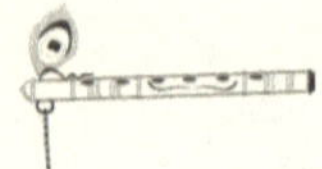

# Love and Nothing

From historic time to the current time, There are countless tales of lovers who have sacrificed their lives for one another or for the one they love just because society forbids them due to the Distinction of Caste system, Status of families, beauty, status let them die together but not live together. Still in this era the same things are happening, and their sacrifices are not valued.

# प्रेम और रुपए

खुद मुख्तार तो मैं चंद रुपए के लिए ही होऊंगी शायद,

प्यार तो मुझे तुम ही से चाहिए।

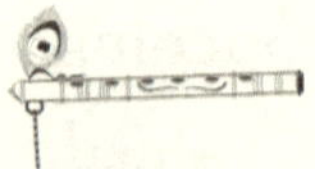

# Love and Money

We often hear the words like "Women are equal to men ", and undoubtedly it is true. Independently she can achieve her sustainability. On another hand this is also true for men.

But what two person seek for them after that sustainability is "the gift of love, care, respect, peace "which is not possible to achieve without being together. Just like our professions, our relationships also demand time and effort.

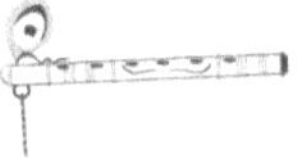

## प्रेम और तकलीफ़

होश अपने भुला कर कहीं

और ही आंख खुलती है,

दर्द दिल का ठहर जाता है कहीं!

जब लाग इश्क़ की लगती है।

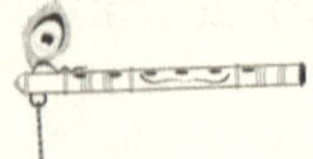



**THE SPEAKING HEART**

# Love and Suffer

A drink of love leaves you entirely in the dream world of your lover. Your mind is overflowing with the thoughts of your lover, and you start thinking about them without any limitation or boundary. Gradually you start becoming like your lover. But when an outbreak occurs, when your lover is not involved in that love as much as you do! This gives rise to unbearable pain, pain that occurs from boundless emotions because when anything crosses its limitation it is harmful.

When you will really fall for someone, you will not be able to resist yourself away from their thoughts!

And that is what binds you up, binds you in a world of dreams.

But when you start expecting the same thing from them, it takes you nearer to pain because in real love there is no place for expectations.

# प्रेम और लालसा

जहां जिस्मानी प्यार की हद खत्म होती है,

वहां रूहानी प्यार की शुरुआत होती है।

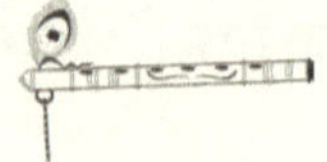

# Love and Lust

Love never starts with lust. Where love of lust ends, their love of soul occurs. Love of soul is eternal, it's without conditions, without expectations, without needs, without thoughts, with everything without everything, here at this stage the love is as pure as nectar but it can never be with lust.

# प्रेम और ढंग

तर्ज़-ए-अबसार ने सीखी है,

दिल ही की बात है!

दिल ही में रखी है।

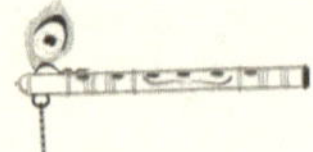

# Love and Manner

Not everyone is able to understand the actual meaning of your words sometime. But with the passage of time you just learn and accept this fact, where you'll come to the decision to not to share your important words with anyone else is a good thing, keeping those words safe within you is best.

# जिंदगी

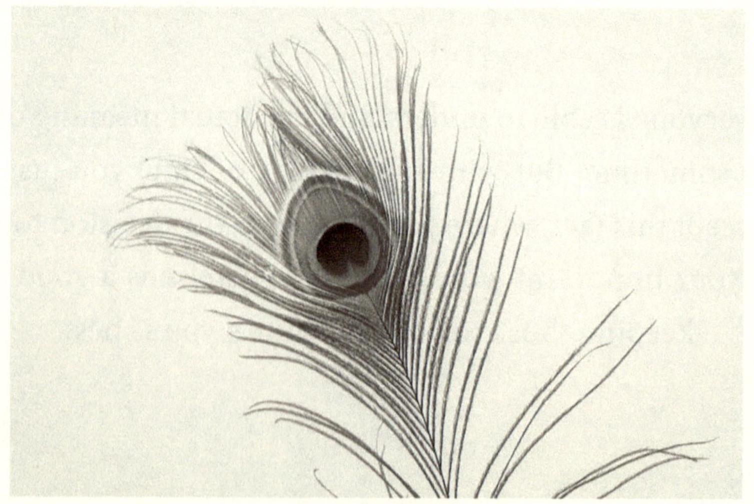

# LIFE

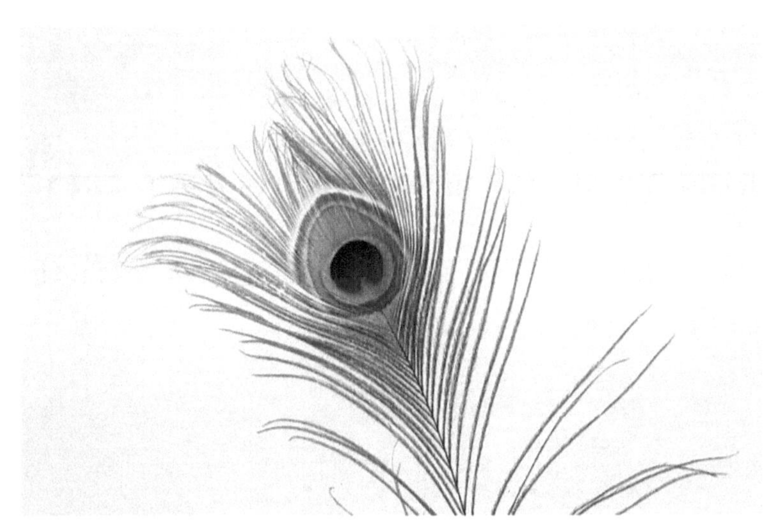

# जिंदगी और बचपन

वो लापरवाही भी अच्छी थी जिसमें सबक तो थे, मगर प्यार भरे!

यह समझदारी तो बात खत्म ही नतीजों पे आ के करती है।

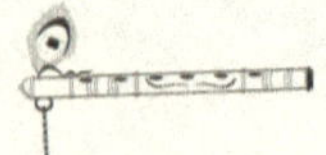

# Life and Childhood

Childhood full of carelessness was the best era where learning came with love. For failing, "appreciation and encouragement to try once again" was the award. Now being grown up, each and every mistake brings consequences with it.

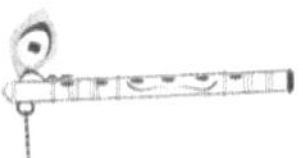

# जिंदगी और समय

ये बुरा वक़्त ही अच्छा है,

ख़ैर मना!

तेरे पास वक़्त तो है।

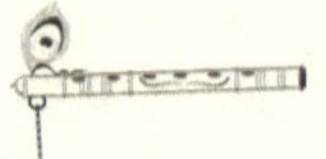

# Life and Time

The natural law of change states that "Time" changes. Nobody lives a life where they just have a good time and never experience hardship. When everything seems to be going well and when our wishes are being fulfilled, we are thankful. However, when a storm of problems suddenly appears, we become ungrateful.

Yet one should know that somewhere on earth - there is someone in a corner who is praying for some extra time to "LIVE" because that someone is depleted and loosing life day-by-day, that someone who is willing to face even the harshest of the moment since all he needs is "time".

So, amid difficult "times," one should be grateful since, as is the law of nature, the storm will soon pass as well.

# जिंदगी और किस्मत

कि! ख्वाहिशों की हंसी अधूरेपन में छुपी है,

फिर मुकम्मल जरूरतों से क्या नाराज़गी ?

जो था मेरा, मेरा था ही नहीं,

फिर खुदा से किस बात की शिक़ायत हुई ?

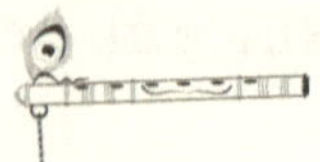

# Life and Destiny

Desire "something that always occurs after fulfillment of wants". Irony is, Desire in words can exist as a 'singular', but throughout life it stands to be 'plural'. The number of desires rises day by day and that number is never ending. And 'reality is we will never be able to fulfill all the desires' and will keep on hurting ourselves. Ignoring the "truth," we continue to dwell on the things we haven't accomplished and fail to express gratitude for what we have. So it's better to stay happy with the things we have, instead feeling sad for the things which we have not achieved.

# जिंदगी और ईमानदारी

आते-जाते मौसम

की तो फितरत है बदलना,

के! इन्सान तो जीने का तरीका समझ बैठा।

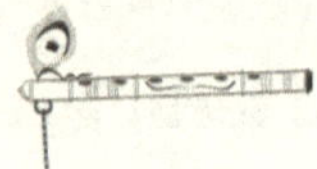

# Life and Honesty

We consistently overlook what nature is trying to teach us and instead we grab onto things that are not necessary. Humans have the ability to think, analyze, examine, and inspect unthinkable things, whereas other beings do not. This is a key distinction between us and other living things. Yet, we actually aren't using it properly. Our minds constantly come up with new ways to increase our income, elevate our status, and gain recognition and fame. In the same manner, the person has no regard for the conditions, sentiments, or emotions for anyone.

# जिंदगी और विचार

बड़ा जोर है इस सोच का,

ना जाने क्या-क्या बांध लेती है,

कीमत कुछ भी नहीं और कीमती भी सब बना देती है।

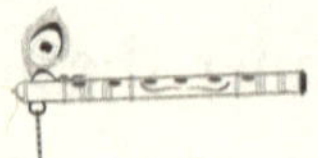

# Life and Thought

A single thought can do anything or nothing. A single thought is a creation, and a single thought is destruction.

Choose it wisely!

# जिंदगी और संघर्ष

छोटी सी उम्र में हालातों से खेला था वो,

लोगों का वेहम था!

रातों रात मशहूर हुआ है वो।

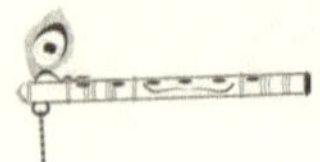

# Life and Struggle

No one becomes successful overnight. Everyone puts forth a lot of effort in the beginning until every cell in their body can smell their sweat. Other person have no idea what challenges they encountered on the way, from how much pain they had suffered through. The successful individual is raised by this entire collaborative effort. But people only see whatever is shown and don't try to find hidden stories behind the hard work.

# जिंदगी और लोग

दुनिया के भीतर ही दु है,

सवाल होगा किस और से ?

ना वाकिफ मैं ना तू है!

-0फ़क़त! तू बस यकीन रख साथी,

नज़रअंदाज़ लोगों को करने का हुनर मुझ में भी खूब है।

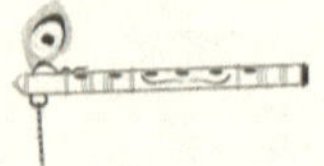

# Life and People

A person from birth, birth to their growth, growth to progress takes each and every decision by keeping so many thoughts in mind like how that decision will affect the family? Or how will society react? what society will say?. Sometimes decisions are taken by listening to the advice of many, sometimes decisions are taken against the will just because there are no other solutions according to us due to the harsh reaction of people. Although that decision might actually not hold any unwanted consequences.

The same thing occurs throughout one's entire life, and the person continues to bury their wishes inside even if that was possible to fulfill. But the moment that person firmly chooses to act in a way that makes him genuinely pleased, that very same day, he fights with everyone and even with his own heart to achieve it. That fight is not easy but in the end it becomes necessary to become a warrior.

# जिंदगी और दोस्त

मुसाहिब हो, मुसाफिर तो नहीं हो जाओगे ?

के! निगाहें जो फेरों कभी,

तो फिर नीयत तो! नहीं बदल जाओगे ?

कि! पल एक ही काफ़ी है,

कि! पल एक ही काफ़ी है,

कहानी नई अगर कोई तुम,

दिल-ए-पन्ने पर लिखना चाहोगे।


मुसाहिब - Close friend.

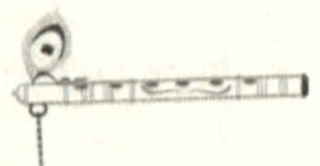

# Life and Friend

There are a lot of people around us on this incredible adventure called life, but only a select few may truly be considered close who we can count. Those countable are really our special one's for some reason. Those reasons are not occur just by the conversations. Those reasons occur when God creates the unwanted situations to show us that how that special one's act, if they will stay as our friends or will turn to be an unknown person, if their behavior remains same or will change with the circumstances. Every time these happens write new words on the very pages of our hearts and create chapters of our life.

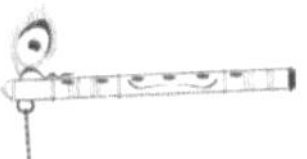

# जिंदगी और सिफ़र

सिर्फ और सिफ़र की ही तो बात है!

क़ीमत तबस्सुम की,

क़ीमत दर्द की।


सिर्फ - only

सिफ़र -zero

तबस्सुम - smile

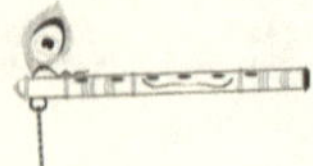

# Life and Zero

There is "only one" that can brings smiles, that can brings sorrows, that can raise the happiness, that can raise the pain. This makes us valuable and at the same time this makes us worthless.

These zero plays throughout the life with us and in last we are again zero.

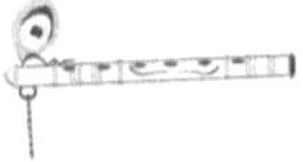

# जिंदगी और क्षमा

मैंने गिले-शिकवों को रिहाई दे दी है,

क्या अब की बार तुम मुस्कुरा के मिलोगे मुझसे ?

अरे! अब तो ख़ुदा ने भी मेरी गवाही दे दी है।

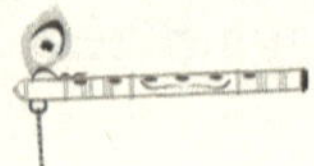

# Life and Forgiveness

Forgive and move forward. Life is long to hold the grief and short to enjoy happiness. Say sorry if it raises positivity and peace inside. Be grateful.

# जिंदगी और यादें

मुरझाए पत्तों में अक्सर यादें मेहका करती हैं,

कैद तस्वीरों में अक्सर कहानियाँ रहा करती हैं।

# Life and Memories

Moments that are captured always contain both happy and sad tales, pleasant greetings and difficult farewells, unpredictable events and unexpected smiles. Those captures are in fact "Treasure".

# जिंदगी और माता-पिता

भूखे तो नहीं सोते जब तक मां है,

महफ़ूज़ हो घर पे जब तक बाप है।

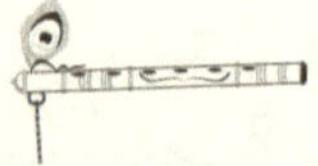

# Love and Parents

No matter what the circumstances are, your mother will never let you go to bed hungry. And our father is the finest safeguard for us; just having him there deters others from harming us.

# जिंदगी और जीना

ये मसरूफ़ सी जिंदगी में मस्त रहा करो,

थोड़ा हसा के किसी को,

थोड़ा खुद हस लिया करो।

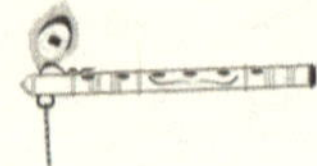

# Life and Living

In this modern era, each and everyone is so busy that no one holds a single minute to look after the situation of the person who is sitting beside them which is leading to problems like depression, anxiety, and misery. So why we are not able to try to make someone smile, why we are not able to make someone stress free at least for some time by hearing their problems and trying.

# जिंदगी और आस्था

सलामती दुआ दिल से कुबूल होती है,

मुकम्मल चाहे सारा जहाँ हो जाए!

पर शहर वही बसता है जहां तेरी हजूरी होती है।

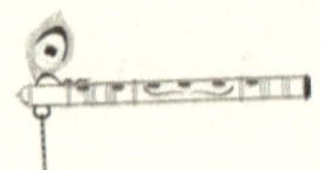

# Life and Devotion

We remember God not because we love him, because we need him, because we hold selfishness in our own interest.!

The Day when we will start loving him without expecting anything from him, we will find him.

# जिंदगी और मुस्कान

कहीं दर्द भी आराम मैं है आज,

कहते काफी वक्त से सहारा लिए जा रहे हो,

अब ज़रा मुस्कुरा के देखो।

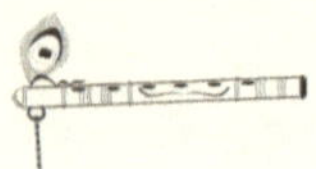

# Life and Smile

Why being sad for the situations that we can't change or control?

Overthinking will take us towards anxiety only due to which we will suffer mentally as well as physically. Instead, we should try to change our attitude towards these situations. Sometimes by becoming negligent like a child, sometimes leaving everything "over a time" - by being patient, sometimes leaving everything in hands of the universe by becoming strong while doing the deeds that are important to be done presently and that are under our control. And while doing all of these things we also have to love ourselves when we will face our hopes shattering, we also have to pamper ourselves when we will feel low and once again, we have to smile with a fire in our heart.

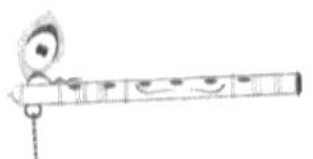

# जिंदगी और बेईमानी

खुद से धोखा करना नहीं छोड़ता इन्सान,

तुम तो फिर ग़ैर हो।

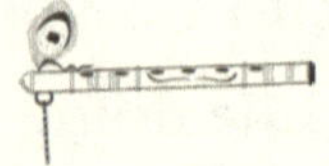

# Life and Cheat

How can we be loyal to someone if we are not true to ourselves?

In situations when we are aware in our hearts that something is not right but still we choose to ignore it since a true "NO" would not be beneficial/or do any good to us whereas a fake "YES" would be acceptable under any circumstances. These things never allow us to expect loyalty from someone else because we are not ready to be truthful with our own heart.

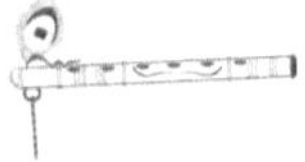

# जिंदगी और चिंता

पहला इंतजार तो चाहत में निकल जाता है और दूसरा चिंता में।

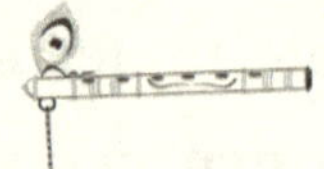

# Life and Overthinking

The first thing is always special. Excitement is always on another level, but we always fail to keep that excitement throughout the journey and there comes the time when it completely vanishes and many things get destroyed and reach to the end without its completion.

# जिंदगी और बोझ

मजबूरी यूं है की पढ़ाई नहीं खुराक़ भाती है,

कोई लाख नया दिन दिखा जाए!

उसकी नज़र में हर वक्त काली रात रहती है।

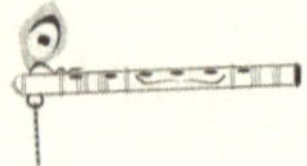

# Life and Stress

Sometimes meeting those people who are unfortunately facing problems like starvation, not having shelter over their head, not having proper clothes to wear, not having clean water to drink leaves us heartbroken. When we decide to help them for improving their "future "they really feel happy and bless us but one agenda that we are not able to achieve in one-time-help is " improvement of their future ", because their problems are so big that your help is not letting them think about their future and they stuck in the happiness of " present". So, we should also try to help in a way where these people should be able to think about their "future".

# जिंदगी और गरीबी

जब किसी गरीब का हक़ मरता है,

तो मारने वाला खुद को बड़ा होशियार समझता है!

मगर वो भूल जाता है की हर चीज़ का हिसाब खुदा रखता है।

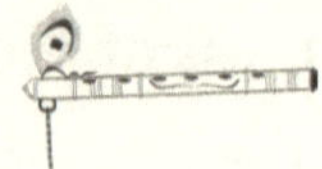

# Life and Poverty

Whatever is wrong, it remains wrong.

No matter if someone is watching you or not.

Keeping honesty to yourself no matter if someone is looking upon you or not, is integrity that should be kept by remembering that We have to pay badly some other day for the fraud we are going to play.

# जिंदगी और सकूं

एक पल बैठ तो जाता,

जिस रोटी केलिए इतना भगा!

उसे परिवार के साथ सकूं से बांट तो लेता।

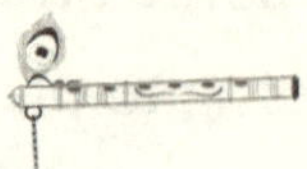

# Life and Peace

Throughout their whole life everyone works hard day and night for the better livelihood of their family.

And forgets that with passing time they are getting old. The time that has gone today will not come back. Then why not try to balance life with work. Collecting moments with the loved ones and spending a happy life with them. Life is so unpredictable that we never know what the next moment will bring in front of us. We never know if the next decision of life will be in our favor or not.

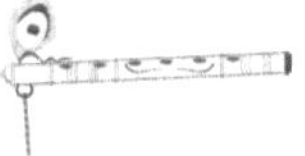

# जिंदगी और मौत

जीवन आकर्षक है!

तभी तो मौत का लंबा सफ़र छोटा लगता है।

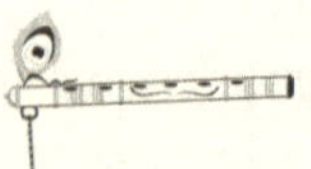

# Life and Death

Living is lie

But still everyone wants to live.

Living is painful.

Living is happiness.

Living is harsh.

Living is amazing.

Collecting everything in life, but then Life ends so fast that we
reach death so soon!

# हृदय

# HEART

# हृदय और प्रार्थना

असर-ए-दवा वक्त पे,

और असर-ए-दुआ बेवक्त!

चंद शब्द,

और जीने केलिए सुकूनत।

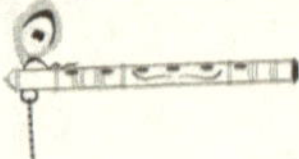

# Heart and Pray

Getting the chance to help someone is a blessing. A blessing that heals you when medicine has no effect exactly at apt time. A blessing that leaves your mind in calmness. A blessing that inspires you to be kind. So, keep helping others.

# हृदय और मनमुटाव


शुक्रिया है हर उस शख़्स का जो मेरे ख़िलाफ हो गया।

बड़ी जिम्मेदारी थी सब के साथ निभाने की!

खैर! अब कुछ बोझ कम हो गया।

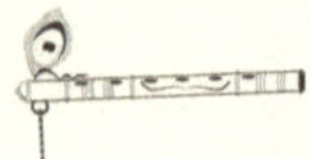

# Heart and Grudges

Be thankful to those also who stood against you.

They've just showed you who they truly are. So many things, so many confusions you possibly have kept inside your heavy heart, but situations.

But now it's been cleared out. You don't have to care about the emotions of fake people. Now Relax! and move on.

# हृदय और दयालुता

चिरागों की रोशनी तुझे,

मेरी पलकों तले अंधेरा रहता है,

तो क्या!

कभी मेरा खोना तेरा अच्छा कर जाए,

दिल से शुक्रिया तेरा, जो मुझे बदले में तू सुकून दे जाता है।

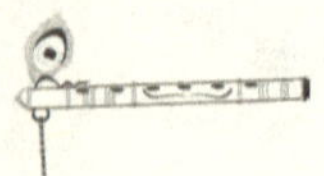

# Heart and Kindness

Try to be a hope for someone.

Try to be someone's happiness.

Try to be someone's Peace.

Because it's really easy to leave someone in pain but it's really hard to take away someone's pain. We never know what someone is going through? but we can be their healer. We can help them in a time of need. Maybe in some situations it will leave us with problems too but maybe our problems will be temporary, and it will be tackle-able.

# ईश्वर

# GOD

# ईश्वर और सब्र

एक सब्र ही तो चाहिए,

गर! खुदा की फ़िक्र चाहिए।

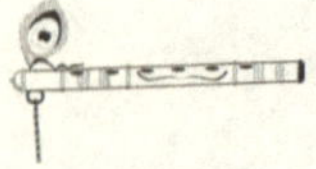

# God and Patience

Nothing can be controlled by ourselves except our "thinking" and it's the toughest deed that can be done by us. Where we will actually stop controlling the situations, the circumstances, the affairs, the states, the surroundings and we will start focusing on taking actions while trying our best to not hurt someone mentally or physically. At same time we will get lesson on how to handle stressful times, hard times, tensions because now we will have one clear statement in our mind that whatever have been decided by Universe it will happen no matter how we are going to react and that's what we need to teach our mind and that's how we will be able to control our mind.

# ईश्वर और प्रेम

सौंप दूं मैं खुद को पूरा तुझे,

पर!

ये! "पर" का ही तो मसला है।

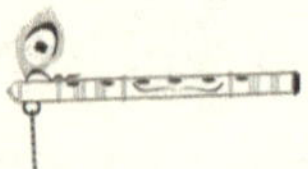

# God and Love

Surrender says "die", die while living (Death while being alive is what surrender means). Whether we are surrendering for love of loved ones or we are surrendering for love of "God". We have to forget "I", "ME"," MYSELF". We only have to find "THEY", "YOU"," YOURS". We have to create a new garden for mankind where plants of "kindness, Generosity, Charity, Courtesy, impartiality will blossom. "I surrender "are not words, these are "whole life", A Life that many want to adopt and stop with the question "BUT"?

# खूबसूरती और भ्रम

चांद जब जमीं पर उतरता है,

तो ग़लत फहमी रखता है।

धोखा ये आंखों का!

और हसीन खुद को समझता है।

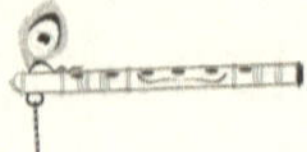

# Beauty and Misunderstanding

What is beauty? What is a body? What's the point of being prettiest? What's the matter with being so classy? If it is not bringing up internal happiness, calmness, relaxation!

And if you are carrying the vanity of it with you just because everyone loves it, then it's the biggest misunderstanding you have.

Your loved ones don't bother about looks, they love you and only you unconditionally no matter how you are, this" love" and "care" actually doesn't have space for your looks. Be ready, be bold, be attractive, be beautiful, be nice looking, be amazing but not for others but for yourself, just for yourself.

# रिश्ता और सब्र

की बस सब्र ही तो रखना है!

रंजिशे भी हैं,

गिले भी हैं,

शिकवे भी हैं,

की बस रिश्ता ही तो रखना है।

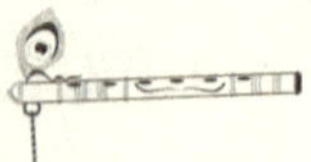

# Relationship and Patience

We all have complaints.

We all have grievances.

We all have problems.

We all have objections.

But we lack the patience necessary to make all the necessary adjustments to maintain the stability of our relationships.

Even if we all forget that no one is flawless, we nevertheless keep pointing out flaws in other people.

# आत्म निर्णय और दुनिया

कितना भागा होऊंगा मैं तुझ तक पहुंचने से पहले,

हर किसी की सलाह,

किसी किसी का मशवरा,

हर बार की मर्जी,

तक़रीबन की मज़बूरी,

पर सोच! ऐ-मेरे दिल!!

कितना लड़ा होऊंगा मैं तुझ ही का फैंसला मानने से पहले।

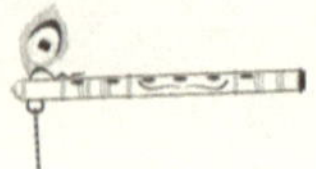

# Self Decision and Society

Sometimes for a person, it really seems hard to take the simple decision.

A decision that the heart asks for!

Sometimes unwanted advices stops, Sometimes unwanted circumstances stops, sometimes unwanted society pressure, pressure which even turns friends, our near ones, loved ones and even "own families too" against the same decision. It really needs power to still stay with that one decision, a power which brings out transformation for one and all.